ELIZABETH II   c. **52**

Mental Health (Patients in the Community) Act 1995

1995 CHAPTER 52

An Act to make provision for certain mentally disordered patients in England and Wales to receive after-care under supervision after leaving hospital; to provide for the making of community care orders in the case of certain mentally disordered patients in Scotland; to amend the law relating to mentally disordered patients absent without leave or on leave of absence from hospital; and for connected purposes. [8th November 1995]

BE IT ENACTED by the Queen's most Excellent Majesty, by and with the advice and consent of the Lords Spiritual and Temporal, and Commons, in this present Parliament assembled, and by the authority of the same, as follows:—

England and Wales

1.—(1) After section 25 of the Mental Health Act 1983 there shall be inserted the following sections—

After-care under supervision.
1983 c. 20.

"After-care under supervision

Application for supervision.

25A.—(1) Where a patient—

    (a) is liable to be detained in a hospital in pursuance of an application for admission for treatment; and

    (b) has attained the age of 16 years,

an application may be made for him to be supervised after he leaves hospital, for the period allowed by the following provisions of this Act, with a view to securing that he receives the after-care services provided for him under section 117 below.

(2) In this Act an application for a patient to be so supervised is referred to as a "supervision application"; and where a supervision application has been duly made

and accepted under this Part of this Act in respect of a patient and he has left hospital, he is for the purposes of this Act "subject to after-care under supervision" (until he ceases to be so subject in accordance with the provisions of this Act).

(3) A supervision application shall be made in accordance with this section and sections 25B and 25C below.

(4) A supervision application may be made in respect of a patient only on the grounds that—

    (a) he is suffering from mental disorder, being mental illness, severe mental impairment, psychopathic disorder or mental impairment;

    (b) there would be a substantial risk of serious harm to the health or safety of the patient or the safety of other persons, or of the patient being seriously exploited, if he were not to receive the after-care services to be provided for him under section 117 below after he leaves hospital; and

    (c) his being subject to after-care under supervision is likely to help to secure that he receives the after-care services to be so provided.

(5) A supervision application may be made only by the responsible medical officer.

(6) A supervision application in respect of a patient shall be addressed to the Health Authority which will have the duty under section 117 below to provide after-care services for the patient after he leaves hospital.

(7) Before accepting a supervision application in respect of a patient a Health Authority shall consult the local social services authority which will also have that duty.

(8) Where a Health Authority accept a supervision application in respect of a patient the Health Authority shall—

    (a) inform the patient both orally and in writing—

        (i) that the supervision application has been accepted; and

        (ii) of the effect in his case of the provisions of this Act relating to a patient subject to after-care under supervision (including, in particular, what rights of applying to a Mental Health Review Tribunal are available);

    (b) inform any person whose name is stated in the supervision application in accordance with sub-paragraph (i) of paragraph (e) of section 25B(5) below that the supervision application has been accepted; and

90 0389346 5

Mental Health (Patients in the Community) Act 1995

CHAPTER 52

ARRANGEMENT OF SECTIONS

(c) inform in writing any person whose name is so stated in accordance with sub-paragraph (ii) of that paragraph that the supervision application has been accepted.

(9) Where a patient in respect of whom a supervision application is made is granted leave of absence from a hospital under section 17 above (whether before or after the supervision application is made), references in—

(a) this section and the following provisions of this Part of this Act; and

(b) Part V of this Act,

to his leaving hospital shall be construed as references to his period of leave expiring (otherwise than on his return to the hospital or transfer to another hospital).

Making of supervision application.

25B.—(1) The responsible medical officer shall not make a supervision application unless—

(a) subsection (2) below is complied with; and

(b) the responsible medical officer has considered the matters specified in subsection (4) below.

(2) This subsection is complied with if—

(a) the following persons have been consulted about the making of the supervision application—

(i) the patient;

(ii) one or more persons who have been professionally concerned with the patient's medical treatment in hospital;

(iii) one or more persons who will be professionally concerned with the after-care services to be provided for the patient under section 117 below; and

(iv) any person who the responsible medical officer believes will play a substantial part in the care of the patient after he leaves hospital but will not be professionally concerned with any of the after-care services to be so provided;

(b) such steps as are practicable have been taken to consult the person (if any) appearing to be the nearest relative of the patient about the making of the supervision application; and

(c) the responsible medical officer has taken into account any views expressed by the persons consulted.

(3) Where the patient has requested that paragraph (b) of subsection (2) above should not apply, that paragraph shall not apply unless—

(a) the patient has a propensity to violent or dangerous behaviour towards others; and

> (b) the responsible medical officer considers that it is appropriate for steps such as are mentioned in that paragraph to be taken.

(4) The matters referred to in subsection (1)(b) above are—

> (a) the after-care services to be provided for the patient under section 117 below; and
>
> (b) any requirements to be imposed on him under section 25D below.

(5) A supervision application shall state—

> (a) that the patient is liable to be detained in a hospital in pursuance of an application for admission for treatment;
>
> (b) the age of the patient or, if his exact age is not known to the applicant, that the patient is believed to have attained the age of 16 years;
>
> (c) that in the opinion of the applicant (having regard in particular to the patient's history) all of the conditions set out in section 25A(4) above are complied with;
>
> (d) the name of the person who is to be the community responsible medical officer, and of the person who is to be the supervisor, in relation to the patient after he leaves hospital; and
>
> (e) the name of—
>
>> (i) any person who has been consulted under paragraph (a)(iv) of subsection (2) above; and
>>
>> (ii) any person who has been consulted under paragraph (b) of that subsection.

(6) A supervision application shall be accompanied by—

> (a) the written recommendation in the prescribed form of a registered medical practitioner who will be professionally concerned with the patient's medical treatment after he leaves hospital or, if no such practitioner other than the responsible medical officer will be so concerned, of any registered medical practitioner; and
>
> (b) the written recommendation in the prescribed form of an approved social worker.

(7) A recommendation under subsection (6)(a) above shall include a statement that in the opinion of the medical practitioner (having regard in particular to the patient's history) all of the conditions set out in section 25A(4) above are complied with.

(8) A recommendation under subsection (6)(b) above shall include a statement that in the opinion of the social

worker (having regard in particular to the patient's history) both of the conditions set out in section 25A(4)(b) and (c) above are complied with.

(9) A supervision application shall also be accompanied by—

    (a) a statement in writing by the person who is to be the community responsible medical officer in relation to the patient after he leaves hospital that he is to be in charge of the medical treatment provided for the patient as part of the after-care services provided for him under section 117 below;

    (b) a statement in writing by the person who is to be the supervisor in relation to the patient after he leaves hospital that he is to supervise the patient with a view to securing that he receives the after-care services so provided;

    (c) details of the after-care services to be provided for the patient under section 117 below; and

    (d) details of any requirements to be imposed on him under section 25D below.

(10) On making a supervision application in respect of a patient the responsible medical officer shall—

    (a) inform the patient both orally and in writing;

    (b) inform any person who has been consulted under paragraph (a)(iv) of subsection (2) above; and

    (c) inform in writing any person who has been consulted under paragraph (b) of that subsection,

of the matters specified in subsection (11) below.

(11) The matters referred to in subsection (10) above are—

    (a) that the application is being made;

    (b) the after-care services to be provided for the patient under section 117 below;

    (c) any requirements to be imposed on him under section 25D below; and

    (d) the name of the person who is to be the community responsible medical officer, and of the person who is to be the supervisor, in relation to the patient after he leaves hospital.

Supervision applications: supplementary.

25C.—(1) Subject to subsection (2) below, a supervision application, and the recommendation under section 25B(6)(a) above accompanying it, may describe the patient as suffering from more than one of the following forms of mental disorder, namely, mental illness, severe mental impairment, psychopathic disorder and mental impairment.

(2) A supervision application shall be of no effect

unless the patient is described in the application and the recommendation under section 25B(6)(a) above accompanying it as suffering from the same form of mental disorder, whether or not he is also described in the application or the recommendation as suffering from another form.

(3) A registered medical practitioner may at any reasonable time visit a patient and examine him in private for the purpose of deciding whether to make a recommendation under section 25B(6)(a) above.

(4) An approved social worker may at any reasonable time visit and interview a patient for the purpose of deciding whether to make a recommendation under section 25B(6)(b) above.

(5) For the purpose of deciding whether to make a recommendation under section 25B(6) above in respect of a patient, a registered medical practitioner or an approved social worker may require the production of and inspect any records relating to the detention or treatment of the patient in any hospital or to any after-care services provided for the patient under section 117 below.

(6) If, within the period of 14 days beginning with the day on which a supervision application has been accepted, the application, or any recommendation accompanying it, is found to be in any respect incorrect or defective, the application or recommendation may, within that period and with the consent of the Health Authority which accepted the application, be amended by the person by whom it was made or given.

(7) Where an application or recommendation is amended in accordance with subsection (6) above it shall have effect, and shall be deemed to have had effect, as if it had been originally made or given as so amended.

(8) A supervision application which appears to be duly made and to be accompanied by recommendations under section 25B(6) above may be acted upon without further proof of—

    (a) the signature or qualification of the person by whom the application or any such recommendation was made or given; or

    (b) any matter of fact or opinion stated in the application or recommendation.

(9) A recommendation under section 25B(6) above accompanying a supervision application in respect of a patient shall not be given by—

    (a) the responsible medical officer;

    (b) a person who receives or has an interest in the receipt of any payments made on account of the maintenance of the patient; or

(c) a close relative of the patient, of any person mentioned in paragraph (a) or (b) above or of a person by whom the other recommendation is given under section 25B(6) above for the purposes of the application.

(10) In subsection (9)(c) above "close relative" means husband, wife, father, father-in-law, mother, mother-in-law, son, son-in-law, daughter, daughter-in-law, brother, brother-in-law, sister or sister-in-law.

Requirements to secure receipt of after-care under supervision.

25D.—(1) Where a patient is subject to after-care under supervision (or, if he has not yet left hospital, is to be so subject after he leaves hospital), the responsible after-care bodies have power to impose any of the requirements specified in subsection (3) below for the purpose of securing that the patient receives the after-care services provided for him under section 117 below.

(2) In this Act "the responsible after-care bodies", in relation to a patient, means the bodies which have (or will have) the duty under section 117 below to provide after-care services for the patient.

(3) The requirements referred to in subsection (1) above are—

(a) that the patient reside at a specified place;

(b) that the patient attend at specified places and times for the purpose of medical treatment, occupation, education or training; and

(c) that access to the patient be given, at any place where the patient is residing, to the supervisor, any registered medical practitioner or any approved social worker or to any other person authorised by the supervisor.

(4) A patient subject to after-care under supervision may be taken and conveyed by, or by any person authorised by, the supervisor to any place where the patient is required to reside or to attend for the purpose of medical treatment, occupation, education or training.

(5) A person who demands—

(a) to be given access to a patient in whose case a requirement has been imposed under subsection (3)(c) above; or

(b) to take and convey a patient in pursuance of subsection (4) above,

shall, if asked to do so, produce some duly authenticated document to show that he is a person entitled to be given access to, or to take and convey, the patient.

Review of after-care under supervision etc.

25E.—(1) The after-care services provided (or to be provided) under section 117 below for a patient who is (or is to be) subject to after-care under supervision, and any requirements imposed on him under section 25D above, shall be kept under review, and (where appropriate) modified, by the responsible after-care bodies.

(2) This subsection applies in relation to a patient who is subject to after-care under supervision where he refuses or neglects—

(a) to receive any or all of the after-care services provided for him under section 117 below; or

(b) to comply with any or all of any requirements imposed on him under section 25D above.

(3) Where subsection (2) above applies in relation to a patient, the responsible after-care bodies shall review, and (where appropriate) modify—

(a) the after-care services provided for him under section 117 below; and

(b) any requirements imposed on him under section 25D above.

(4) Where subsection (2) above applies in relation to a patient, the responsible after-care bodies shall also—

(a) consider whether it might be appropriate for him to cease to be subject to after-care under supervision and, if they conclude that it might be, inform the community responsible medical officer; and

(b) consider whether it might be appropriate for him to be admitted to a hospital for treatment and, if they conclude that it might be, inform an approved social worker.

(5) The responsible after-care bodies shall not modify—

(a) the after-care services provided (or to be provided) under section 117 below for a patient who is (or is to be) subject to after-care under supervision; or

(b) any requirements imposed on him under section 25D above,

unless subsection (6) below is complied with.

(6) This subsection is complied with if—

(a) the patient has been consulted about the modifications;

(b) any person who the responsible after-care bodies believe plays (or will play) a substantial part in the care of the patient but is not (or will not be) professionally concerned with the after-care services provided for the patient under section 117 below has been consulted about the modifications;

(c) such steps as are practicable have been taken to consult the person (if any) appearing to be the nearest relative of the patient about the modifications; and

(d) the responsible after-care bodies have taken into account any views expressed by the persons consulted.

(7) Where the patient has requested that paragraph (c) of subsection (6) above should not apply, that paragraph shall not apply unless—

(a) the patient has a propensity to violent or dangerous behaviour towards others; and

(b) the community responsible medical officer (or the person who is to be the community responsible medical officer) considers that it is appropriate for steps such as are mentioned in that paragraph to be taken.

(8) Where the responsible after-care bodies modify the after-care services provided (or to be provided) for the patient under section 117 below or any requirements imposed on him under section 25D above, they shall—

(a) inform the patient both orally and in writing;

(b) inform any person who has been consulted under paragraph (b) of subsection (6) above; and

(c) inform in writing any person who has been consulted under paragraph (c) of that subsection,

that the modifications have been made.

(9) Where—

(a) a person other than the person named in the supervision application becomes the community responsible medical officer when the patient leaves hospital; or

(b) when the patient is subject to after-care under supervision, one person ceases to be, and another becomes, the community responsible medical officer,

the responsible after-care bodies shall comply with subsection (11) below.

(10) Where—

(a) a person other than the person named in the supervision application becomes the supervisor when the patient leaves hospital; or

(b) when the patient is subject to after-care under supervision, one person ceases to be, and another becomes, the supervisor,

the responsible after-care bodies shall comply with subsection (11) below.

(11) The responsible after-care bodies comply with this subsection if they—

(a) inform the patient both orally and in writing;

(b) inform any person who they believe plays a substantial part in the care of the patient but is not professionally concerned with the after-care services provided for the patient under section 117 below; and

(c) unless the patient otherwise requests, take such steps as are practicable to inform in writing the person (if any) appearing to be the nearest relative of the patient,

of the name of the person who becomes the community responsible medical officer or the supervisor.

Reclassification of patient subject to after-care under supervision.

25F.—(1) If it appears to the community responsible medical officer that a patient subject to after-care under supervision is suffering from a form of mental disorder other than the form or forms specified in the supervision application made in respect of the patient, he may furnish a report to that effect to the Health Authority which have the duty under section 117 below to provide after-care services for the patient.

(2) Where a report is so furnished the supervision application shall have effect as if that other form of mental disorder were specified in it.

(3) Unless no-one other than the community responsible medical officer is professionally concerned with the patient's medical treatment, he shall consult one or more persons who are so concerned before furnishing a report under subsection (1) above.

(4) Where a report is furnished under subsection (1) above in respect of a patient, the responsible after-care bodies shall—

(a) inform the patient both orally and in writing; and

(b) unless the patient otherwise requests, take such steps as are practicable to inform in writing the person (if any) appearing to be the nearest relative of the patient,

that the report has been furnished.

Duration and renewal of after-care under supervision.

25G.—(1) Subject to sections 25H and 25I below, a patient subject to after-care under supervision shall be so subject for the period—

(a) beginning when he leaves hospital; and

(b) ending with the period of six months beginning with the day on which the supervision application was accepted,

but shall not be so subject for any longer period except in accordance with the following provisions of this section.

(2) A patient already subject to after-care under supervision may be made so subject—

(a) from the end of the period referred to in subsection (1) above, for a further period of six months; and

(b) from the end of any period of renewal under paragraph (a) above, for a further period of one year,

and so on for periods of one year at a time.

(3) Within the period of two months ending on the day on which a patient who is subject to after-care under supervision would (in default of the operation of subsection (7) below) cease to be so subject, it shall be the duty of the community responsible medical officer—

(a) to examine the patient; and

(b) if it appears to him that the conditions set out in subsection (4) below are complied with, to furnish to the responsible after-care bodies a report to that effect in the prescribed form.

(4) The conditions referred to in subsection (3) above are that—

(a) the patient is suffering from mental disorder, being mental illness, severe mental impairment, psychopathic disorder or mental impairment;

(b) there would be a substantial risk of serious harm to the health or safety of the patient or the safety of other persons, or of the patient being seriously exploited, if he were not to receive the after-care services provided for him under section 117 below;

(c) his being subject to after-care under supervision is likely to help to secure that he receives the after-care services so provided.

(5) The community responsible medical officer shall not consider whether the conditions set out in subsection (4) above are complied with unless—

(a) the following persons have been consulted—

(i) the patient;

(ii) the supervisor;

(iii) unless no-one other than the community responsible medical officer is professionally concerned with the patient's medical treatment, one or more persons who are so concerned;

(iv) one or more persons who are professionally concerned with the after-care services (other than medical treatment) provided for the patient under section 117 below; and

(v) any person who the community responsible medical officer believes plays a substantial part in the care of the patient but is not professionally concerned with the after-care services so provided;

(b) such steps as are practicable have been taken to consult the person (if any) appearing to be the nearest relative of the patient; and

(c) the community responsible medical officer has taken into account any relevant views expressed by the persons consulted.

(6) Where the patient has requested that paragraph (b) of subsection (5) above should not apply, that paragraph shall not apply unless—

(a) the patient has a propensity to violent or dangerous behaviour towards others; and

(b) the community responsible medical officer considers that it is appropriate for steps such as are mentioned in that paragraph to be taken.

(7) Where a report is duly furnished under subsection (3) above, the patient shall be thereby made subject to after-care under supervision for the further period prescribed in that case by subsection (2) above.

(8) Where a report is furnished under subsection (3) above, the responsible after-care bodies shall—

(a) inform the patient both orally and in writing—

(i) that the report has been furnished; and

(ii) of the effect in his case of the provisions of this Act relating to making a patient subject to after-care under supervision for a further period (including, in particular, what rights of applying to a Mental Health Review Tribunal are available);

(b) inform any person who has been consulted under paragraph (a)(v) of subsection (5) above that the report has been furnished; and

(c) inform in writing any person who has been consulted under paragraph (b) of that subsection that the report has been furnished.

(9) Where the form of mental disorder specified in a report furnished under subsection (3) above is a form of disorder other than that specified in the supervision application, that application shall have effect as if that other form of mental disorder were specified in it.

(10) Where on any occasion a report specifying such a form of mental disorder is furnished under subsection (3) above the community responsible medical officer need not on that occasion furnish a report under section 25F above.

Ending of after-care under supervision.

25H.—(1) The community responsible medical officer may at any time direct that a patient subject to after-care under supervision shall cease to be so subject.

(2) The community responsible medical officer shall not give a direction under subsection (1) above unless subsection (3) below is complied with.

(3) This subsection is complied with if—

(a) the following persons have been consulted about the giving of the direction—

(i) the patient;

(ii) the supervisor;

(ii) unless no-one other than the community responsible medical officer is professionally concerned with the patient's medical treatment, one or more persons who are so concerned;

(iv) one or more persons who are professionally concerned with the after-care services (other than medical treatment) provided for the patient under section 117 below; and

(v) any person who the community responsible medical officer believes plays a substantial part in the care of the patient but is not professionally concerned with the after-care services so provided;

(b) such steps as are practicable have been taken to consult the person (if any) appearing to be the nearest relative of the patient about the giving of the direction; and

(c) the community responsible medical officer has taken into account any views expressed by the persons consulted.

(4) Where the patient has requested that paragraph (b) of subsection (3) above should not apply, that paragraph shall not apply unless—

(a) the patient has a propensity to violent or dangerous behaviour towards others; and

(b) the community responsible medical officer considers that it is appropriate for steps such as are mentioned in that paragraph to be taken.

(5) A patient subject to after-care under supervision shall cease to be so subject if he—

(a) is admitted to a hospital in pursuance of an application for admission for treatment; or

(b) is received into guardianship.

(6) Where a patient (for any reason) ceases to be subject to after-care under supervision the responsible after-care bodies shall—

(a) inform the patient both orally and in writing;

    (b) inform any person who they believe plays a substantial part in the care of the patient but is not professionally concerned with the after-care services provided for the patient under section 117 below; and

    (c) take such steps as are practicable to inform in writing the person (if any) appearing to be the nearest relative of the patient,

that the patient has ceased to be so subject.

    (7) Where the patient has requested that paragraph (c) of subsection (6) above should not apply, that paragraph shall not apply unless subsection (3)(b) above applied in his case by virtue of subsection (4) above.

Special provisions as to patients sentenced to imprisonment etc.
    25I.—(1) This section applies where a patient who is subject to after-care under supervision—

    (a) is detained in custody in pursuance of any sentence or order passed or made by a court in the United Kingdom (including an order committing or remanding him in custody); or

    (b) is detained in hospital in pursuance of an application for admission for assessment.

    (2) At any time when the patient is detained as mentioned in subsection (1)(a) or (b) above he is not required—

    (a) to receive any after-care services provided for him under section 117 below; or

    (b) to comply with any requirements imposed on him under section 25D above.

    (3) If the patient is detained as mentioned in paragraph (a) of subsection (1) above for a period of, or successive periods amounting in the aggregate to, six months or less, or is detained as mentioned in paragraph (b) of that subsection, and, apart from this subsection, he—

    (a) would have ceased to be subject to after-care under supervision during the period for which he is so detained; or

    (b) would cease to be so subject during the period of 28 days beginning with the day on which he ceases to be so detained,

he shall be deemed not to have ceased, and shall not cease, to be so subject until the end of that period of 28 days.

    (4) Where the period for which the patient is subject to after-care under supervision is extended by subsection (3) above, any examination and report to be made and furnished in respect of the patient under section 25G(3) above may be made and furnished within the period as so extended.

    (5) Where, by virtue of subsection (4) above, the patient is made subject to after-care under supervision for a further period after the day on which (apart from

subsection (3) above) he would have ceased to be so subject, the further period shall be deemed to have commenced with that day.

Patients moving from Scotland to England and Wales.

25J.—(1) A supervision application may be made in respect of a patient who is subject to a community care order under the Mental Health (Scotland) Act 1984 and who intends to leave Scotland in order to reside in England and Wales.

1984 c. 36.

(2) Sections 25A to 25I above, section 117 below and any other provision of this Act relating to supervision applications or patients subject to after-care under supervision shall apply in relation to a patient in respect of whom a supervision application is or is to be made by virtue of this section subject to such modifications as the Secretary of State may by regulations prescribe."

(2) Schedule 1 to this Act (supplementary provisions about after-care under supervision) shall have effect.

2.—(1) In section 18 of the Mental Health Act 1983 (return of patients absent without leave), for subsection (4) (which provides that a patient may not be taken into custody after the end of the period of 28 days beginning with the first day of his absence without leave) there shall be substituted the following subsection—

Absence without leave.

1983 c. 20.

"(4) A patient shall not be taken into custody under this section after the later of—

(a) the end of the period of six months beginning with the first day of his absence without leave; and

(b) the end of the period for which (apart from section 21 below) he is liable to be detained or subject to guardianship;

and, in determining for the purposes of paragraph (b) above or any other provision of this Act whether a person who is or has been absent without leave is at any time liable to be detained or subject to guardianship, a report furnished under section 20 or 21B below before the first day of his absence without leave shall not be taken to have renewed the authority for his detention or guardianship unless the period of renewal began before that day."

(2) For section 21 of that Act (duration of authority for detention and guardianship: special provisions as to patients absent without leave) there shall be substituted the following sections—

"Special provisions as to patients absent without leave.

21.—(1) Where a patient is absent without leave—

(a) on the day on which (apart from this section) he would cease to be liable to be detained or subject to guardianship under this Part of this Act; or

(b) within the period of one week ending with that day,

he shall not cease to be so liable or subject until the relevant time.

(2) For the purposes of subsection (1) above the relevant time—

(a) where the patient is taken into custody under section 18 above, is the end of the period of one week beginning with the day on which he is returned to the hospital or place where he ought to be;

(b) where the patient returns himself to the hospital or place where he ought to be within the period during which he can be taken into custody under section 18 above, is the end of the period of one week beginning with the day on which he so returns himself; and

(c) otherwise, is the end of the period during which he can be taken into custody under section 18 above.

Patients who are taken into custody or return within 28 days.

21A.—(1) This section applies where a patient who is absent without leave is taken into custody under section 18 above, or returns himself to the hospital or place where he ought to be, not later than the end of the period of 28 days beginning with the first day of his absence without leave.

(2) Where the period for which the patient is liable to be detained or subject to guardianship is extended by section 21 above, any examination and report to be made and furnished in respect of the patient under section 20(3) or (6) above may be made and furnished within the period as so extended.

(3) Where the authority for the detention or guardianship of the patient is renewed by virtue of subsection (2) above after the day on which (apart from section 21 above) that authority would have expired, the renewal shall take effect as from that day.

Patients who are taken into custody or return after more than 28 days.

21B.—(1) This section applies where a patient who is absent without leave is taken into custody under section 18 above, or returns himself to the hospital or place where he ought to be, later than the end of the period of 28 days beginning with the first day of his absence without leave.

(2) It shall be the duty of the appropriate medical officer, within the period of one week beginning with the day on which the patient is returned or returns himself to the hospital or place where he ought to be—

(a) to examine the patient; and

(b) if it appears to him that the relevant conditions are satisfied, to furnish to the appropriate body a report to that effect in the prescribed form;

and where such a report is furnished in respect of the patient the appropriate body shall cause him to be informed.

(3) Where the patient is liable to be detained (as opposed to subject to guardianship), the appropriate medical officer shall, before furnishing a report under subsection (2) above, consult—

(a) one or more other persons who have been professionally concerned with the patient's medical treatment; and

(b) an approved social worker.

(4) Where the patient would (apart from any renewal of the authority for his detention or guardianship on or after the day on which he is returned or returns himself to the hospital or place where he ought to be) be liable to be detained or subject to guardianship after the end of the period of one week beginning with that day, he shall cease to be so liable or subject at the end of that period unless a report is duly furnished in respect of him under subsection (2) above.

(5) Where the patient would (apart from section 21 above) have ceased to be liable to be detained or subject to guardianship on or before the day on which a report is duly furnished in respect of him under subsection (2) above, the report shall renew the authority for his detention or guardianship for the period prescribed in that case by section 20(2) above.

(6) Where the authority for the detention or guardianship of the patient is renewed by virtue of subsection (5) above—

(a) the renewal shall take effect as from the day on which (apart from section 21 above and that subsection) the authority would have expired; and

(b) if (apart from this paragraph) the renewed authority would expire on or before the day on which the report is furnished, the report shall further renew the authority, as from the day on which it would expire, for the period prescribed in that case by section 20(2) above.

(7) Where the authority for the detention or guardianship of the patient would expire within the period of two months beginning with the day on which a report is duly furnished in respect of him under subsection (2) above, the report shall, if it so provides, have effect also as a report duly furnished under section 20(3) or (6) above; and the reference in this subsection to authority includes any authority renewed under subsection (5) above by the report.

(8) Where the form of mental disorder specified in a report furnished under subsection (2) above is a form of disorder other than that specified in the application for admission for treatment or guardianship application concerned (and the report does not have effect as a report furnished under section 20(3) or (6) above), that application shall have effect as if that other form of mental disorder were specified in it.

(9) Where on any occasion a report specifying such a form of mental disorder is furnished under subsection (2) above the appropriate medical officer need not on that occasion furnish a report under section 16 above.

(10) In this section—

"appropriate medical officer" has the same meaning as in section 16(5) above;

"the appropriate body" means—

(a) in relation to a patient who is liable to be detained in a hospital, the managers of the hospital; and

(b) in relation to a patient who is subject to guardianship, the responsible local social services authority; and

"the relevant conditions" means—

(a) in relation to a patient who is liable to be detained in a hospital, the conditions set out in subsection (4) of section 20 above; and

(b) in relation to a patient who is subject to guardianship, the conditions set out in subsection (7) of that section."

(3) In section 22 of that Act (special provisions as to patients sentenced to imprisonment etc.)—

(a) in subsection (2) (detained patient in whose case application for admission for treatment or guardianship application does not cease to have effect), for the words "and 21" there shall be substituted ", 21 and 21A"; and

(b) after that subsection there shall be inserted the following subsection—

"(3) In its application by virtue of subsection (2) above section 18(4) above shall have effect with the substitution of the words "end of the period of 28 days beginning with the first day of his absence without leave." for the words from "later of" onwards."

(4) In section 40 of that Act (effect of hospital orders and guardianship orders), after subsection (5) there shall be inserted the following subsection—

"(6) Where—

(a) a patient admitted to a hospital in pursuance of a hospital order is absent without leave;

(b) a warrant to arrest him has been issued under section 72 of the Criminal Justice Act 1967; and

1967 c. 80.

(c) he is held pursuant to the warrant in any country or territory other than the United Kingdom, any of the Channel Islands and the Isle of Man,

he shall be treated as having been taken into custody under section 18 above on first being so held."

(5) In section 61 of that Act (review of treatment), in subsection (1) (report on treatment and patient's condition to be given to Secretary of

State), in paragraph (a) (report to be given when report furnished under section 20(3)), for the words "in respect of the patient under section 20(3) above" there shall be substituted "under section 20(3) or 21B(2) above renewing the authority for the detention of the patient".

(6) In section 66 of that Act (applications to tribunals)—

(a) in subsection (1) (cases where application may be made), after paragraph (f) there shall be inserted the following paragraphs—

"(fa) a report is furnished under subsection (2) of section 21B above in respect of a patient and subsection (5) of that section applies (or subsections (5) and (6)(b) of that section apply) in the case of the report; or

(fb) a report is furnished under subsection (2) of section 21B above in respect of a patient and subsection (8) of that section applies in the case of the report; or"; and

(b) in subsection (2) (period within which application may be made), in paragraph (d), after "(d)" there shall be inserted ", (fb)" and, in paragraph (f), for the words "of that subsection, the period" there shall be substituted "or (fa) of that subsection, the period or periods".

(7) In section 68 of that Act (duty of managers of hospitals to refer cases to tribunal), in subsection (2) (reference where detention is renewed under section 20 and three years have elapsed since last consideration of case), after "20" there shall be inserted "or 21B".

(8) In Schedule 1 to that Act (application of provisions to patients subject to hospital and guardianship orders), in Part I (patients not subject to special restrictions), in paragraph 1 (provisions applying without modification), for "21," there shall be substituted "21 to 21B,".

3.—(1) In section 17 of the Mental Health Act 1983 (leave of absence for patient liable to be detained in a hospital under Part II of that Act), in subsection (5), the words from "; and without prejudice" to the end (which cause a patient on leave of absence to cease to be liable to be so detained six months after the beginning of his absence even though he would not otherwise have by then ceased to be so liable) shall be omitted. *Leave of absence from hospital.* *1983 c. 20.*

(2) In Schedule 1 to that Act (application of provisions to patients subject to hospital and guardianship orders), in Part II (patients subject to special restrictions), in paragraph 3(c) (modifications of section 17(5)), for the word "six" there shall be substituted "twelve".

(3) Subsections (1) and (2) apply where leave of absence has been granted to a patient before the day on which this section comes into force (as well as where it is granted to a patient after that day).

Scotland

4.—(1) After section 35 of the Mental Health (Scotland) Act 1984 there shall be inserted the following sections— *Community care orders.* *1984 c. 36.*

"Community care orders

Community care orders. 35A.—(1) As respects a patient who is liable to be detained in a hospital in pursuance of an application for admission the responsible medical officer may, in accordance with section 35B of this Act, make an application (in this Act referred to as a "community care application") to the sheriff for an order (in this Act referred to as a "community care order") providing that the patient shall, instead of continuing to be liable to be so detained, be subject to the conditions specified in the order, being conditions imposed with a view to ensuring that he receives—

(a) medical treatment; and

(b) after-care services provided for him under section 8 of this Act.

(2) Sections 21(1), (2)(a) and (b), (3), (4) and (5) and 113 of this Act shall apply with respect to a community care application as they apply with respect to an application for admission.

(3) The sheriff shall, as respects a community care application—

(a) make a community care order in respect of the patient, subject to the conditions set out in the application or to such other conditions as the sheriff considers appropriate; or

(b) refuse the application.

(4) A community care order shall specify—

(a) the conditions to which the patient is to be subject;

(b) the name of the medical practitioner (the "special medical officer") who is to be principally concerned with the patient's medical treatment while the order is in force, who shall be a practitioner approved for the purposes of section 20 of this Act by a Health Board as having special experience in the diagnosis or treatment of mental disorder; and

(c) the name of the person (the "after-care officer") who is to be responsible for co-ordinating the provision of the after-care services to be provided for the patient under section 8 of this Act while the order is in force, who shall be a mental health officer of the local authority which is to provide the after-care services to be so provided.

(5) The sheriff may defer the making of a community care order until such arrangements as appear to him to be necessary for the provision of medical treatment and after-care services to the patient following the making of the order have been made to the sheriff's satisfaction.

(6) If, on the date when a patient ceases to be liable to be detained in a hospital in pursuance of an application for admission, a community care application has been made in respect of him but has not been determined, his

liability to be so detained shall continue until the community care order comes into force or, as the case may be, the application is refused by the sheriff.

(7) If, on the date when a patient ceases to be liable to be detained in a hospital in pursuance of an application for admission, a community care order has been made in respect of him but has not come into force, his liability to be so detained shall continue until the order comes into force.

(8) On the coming into force of a community care order in respect of a patient, he shall cease to be liable to be detained in a hospital under this Part of this Act.

(9) The responsible medical officer shall, within 7 days of the making of a community care order, send a copy of the order to—

    (a) the patient and any other person who has been consulted under subsection (3)(a) or (f) or (4) of section 35B of this Act;

    (b) the Mental Welfare Commission;

    (c) the patient's special medical officer; and

    (d) the patient's after-care officer.

(10) The patient's after-care officer shall, on receiving a copy of the community care order, take such steps as are practicable to explain to the patient, both orally and in writing—

    (a) the purpose and effect of the order and of the conditions specified in it;

    (b) the patient's right of appeal to the sheriff under section 35F of this Act; and

    (c) that the patient may make representations to the Mental Welfare Commission,

and shall send a copy of any written explanation to any other person who has been consulted under subsection (3)(a) or (4) of section 35B of this Act.

Community care applications. 35B.—(1) A community care application may be made at any time after the expiry of the period of 28 days beginning with the day on which the patient was admitted to a hospital in pursuance of an application for admission.

(2) Before making a community care application the responsible medical officer shall—

    (a) consult the persons specified in subsection (3) below; and

    (b) consider the matters specified in subsection (5) below.

(3) The persons referred to in subsection (2)(a) above are—

    (a) the patient and, if practicable and the patient does not object, his nearest relative;

(b) the persons who have been principally concerned with the patient's medical treatment in hospital;

(c) the medical practitioner who is to be the patient's special medical officer and the other persons who are to be concerned with the patient's medical treatment after the community care order comes into force;

(d) the person who is to be the patient's after-care officer;

(e) each other person who the responsible medical officer believes is to have a continuing professional involvement in any aspect of the after-care services which are to be provided for the patient under section 8 of this Act after the order comes into force; and

(f) any person who the responsible medical officer believes will play a substantial part in the care of the patient after the order comes into force but will not be professionally concerned with the after-care services to be so provided.

(4) If the patient has a propensity to violent or dangerous behaviour the responsible medical officer may consult the patient's nearest relative notwithstanding any objection by the patient to such consultation under subsection (3)(a) above.

(5) The matters referred to in subsection (2)(b) above are—

(a) the after-care services mentioned in subsection (3)(e) above; and

(b) the conditions which should be specified in the order with a view to ensuring that the patient receives medical treatment and such after-care services.

(6) A community care application shall be in the prescribed form and shall include—

(a) the conditions which the responsible medical officer considers should be specified in the community care order for the purpose mentioned in subsection (5)(b) above;

(b) the name of the medical practitioner who is to be the patient's special medical officer after the order comes into force;

(c) the name of the person who is to be the patient's after-care officer after the order comes into force; and

(d) subject to section 35C(1) of this Act, the period for which the responsible medical officer considers the order should have effect.

(7) A community care application shall be accompanied by—

   (a) two medical recommendations, in the prescribed form and complying with subsection (8) below, one of which shall be given by a medical practitioner approved for the purposes of section 20 of this Act by a Health Board as having special experience in the diagnosis or treatment of mental disorder and the other of which shall, if practicable, be given by another medical practitioner who has previous acquaintance with the patient; and

   (b) a report in the prescribed form from the person who is to be the patient's after-care officer after the order comes into force, and complying with subsection (9) below.

(8) The medical recommendations referred to in subsection (7)(a) above shall consist of statements of opinion that both the following conditions are satisfied, namely—

   (a) that the patient is suffering from mental disorder of a nature or degree which makes it appropriate for him to receive medical treatment, but that the grounds set out in section 17(1) of this Act for admission to and detention in a hospital do not apply to the patient; and

   (b) that the patient requires to be subject to a community care order—

      (i) with a view to ensuring that he receives medical treatment and the after-care services to be provided for him under section 8 of this Act; and

      (ii) in the interests of his health or safety or with a view to the protection of other persons;

and for the purposes of subsection (7)(a) above the recommendations do not comply with this subsection unless the patient is described in each of them as suffering from the same form of mental disorder (that is to say, mental illness or mental handicap), whether or not he is described in either recommendation as suffering also from the other form.

(9) The report referred to in subsection (7)(b) above shall include—

   (a) information as to—

      (i) the patient's social circumstances;

      (ii) the after-care services which are to be provided for the patient under section 8 of this Act after the order comes into force;

      (iii) the care, other than medical treatment and the after-care services so provided, which is to be provided for the patient after the order comes into force; and

(b) a statement that in the opinion of the person making the report the patient requires to be subject to a community care order—

   (i) with a view to ensuring that he receives medical treatment and the after-care services to be so provided; and

   (ii) in the interests of his health or safety or with a view to the protection of other persons.

(10) Before making a community care application the responsible medical officer shall take such steps as are reasonably practicable to inform any person, other than the patient, who has been consulted under subsection (3)(a) or (4) above of his right, by virtue of section 35A(2) of this Act, to be heard by the sheriff regarding the proposed community care order.

Duration and renewal of community care order.

35C.—(1) Subject to section 35J of this Act and the following provisions of this section, a community care order shall have effect for such period, not exceeding 6 months, as may be specified in the order.

(2) A community care order may be renewed under this section—

(a) from the expiry of the period referred to in subsection (1) above, for a further period not exceeding 6 months;

(b) from the expiry of any period of renewal under paragraph (a) above, for a further period not exceeding one year, and so on for periods not exceeding one year at a time.

(3) The special medical officer shall, within the period of two months ending with the day on which the community care order, if not renewed, would expire—

(a) examine the patient; and

(b) consult—

   (i) the patient and, if practicable and the patient does not object, his nearest relative;

   (ii) the patient's after-care officer;

   (iii) the other persons concerned with the patient's medical treatment or professionally concerned with any aspect of the after-care services provided for him under section 8 of this Act; and

   (iv) any person who the special medical officer believes plays a substantial part in the care of the patient but is not professionally concerned with the after-care services so provided.

(4) If the patient has a propensity to violent or dangerous behaviour the responsible medical officer may consult the patient's nearest relative notwithstanding any objection by the patient to such consultation under subsection (3)(b)(i) above.

(5) If, after the examination and consultation required by subsection (3) above and any consultation under subsection (4) above, the special medical officer considers that the conditions set out in section 35B(8)(a) and (b) of this Act continue to apply to the patient, he shall send to the Mental Welfare Commission a report to that effect in the prescribed form, and the community care order shall thereby be renewed for such period as is, subject to subsection (2) above, specified in the report.

(6) The special medical officer shall notify—

(a) the patient and any other person who has been consulted under subsection (3)(b)(i) or (iv) or (4) above; and

(b) the patient's after-care officer,

of any renewal of the community care order and of the period of such renewal.

(7) Subsection (10) of section 35A of this Act shall apply in relation to a renewal of a community care order under this section as it applies in relation to a community care order made under that section, but with the substitution of references to subsections (3)(b)(i) and (4) of this section for the references to subsections (3)(a) and (4) of section 35B.

Variation of conditions in community care order.

35D.—(1) This section applies where the special medical officer, after consulting—

(a) the patient and, if practicable and the patient does not object, his nearest relative;

(b) the other persons concerned with the patient's medical treatment;

(c) the patient's after-care officer;

(d) the other persons professionally concerned with any aspect of the after-care services provided for the patient under section 8 of this Act; and

(e) any person who the special medical officer believes plays a substantial part in the care of the patient but is not professionally concerned with the after-care services so provided,

considers that the conditions specified in the order should be varied (whether by adding further conditions or deleting or amending existing conditions).

(2) If the patient has a propensity to violent or dangerous behaviour the special medical officer may consult the patient's nearest relative notwithstanding any objection by the patient to such consultation under subsection (1)(a) above.

(3) Where this section applies the special medical officer shall prepare a note, in the prescribed form, of the proposed variation of the conditions and shall send a copy of the note to—

(a) the patient and any other person who has been consulted under subsection (1)(a) or (2) above;

(b) the patient's after-care officer; and

(c) the sheriff clerk for the sheriff of the sheriffdom within which the patient is resident.

(4) If the patient wishes to object to or make representations concerning the proposed variation of the conditions he shall, within 7 days of receiving the copy of the note under subsection (3) above, so advise the sheriff clerk; and in that event the sheriff shall not approve the variation without holding a hearing.

(5) If the patient does not indicate, in accordance with subsection (4) above, that he wishes to be heard concerning the proposed variation of the conditions the sheriff shall, if he thinks fit, approve the variation without a hearing.

(6) Where a variation of conditions is approved under this section the special medical officer shall send a copy of the variation as so approved to—

(a) the patient and any other person who has been consulted under subsection (1)(a) or (e) or (2) above;

(b) the Mental Welfare Commission; and

(c) the patient's after-care officer.

(7) Subsection (10) of section 35A of this Act shall apply in relation to a variation of conditions approved under this section as it applies in relation to a community care order made under that section, but with the substitution of references to subsections (1)(a) and (2) of this section for the references to subsections (3)(a) and (4) of section 35B.

Change of special medical officer or after-care officer.

35E.—(1) This subsection applies where a patient's special medical officer, after consulting the persons mentioned in subsection (3) below, agrees with another medical practitioner ("the new special medical officer"), who shall be a practitioner approved for the purposes of section 20 of this Act by a Health Board as having special experience in the diagnosis or treatment of mental disorder, that the new special medical officer should, from a date so agreed, assume principal responsibility for the patient's medical treatment while the community care order is in force.

(2) This subsection applies where a patient's after-care officer, after consulting the persons mentioned in subsection (4) below, agrees with another person ("the new after-care officer"), who shall be a mental health officer of the local authority which is providing (or, if different, the local authority which is to provide) the after-care services to be provided for the patient under section 8 of this Act while the community care order is in force,

that the new after-care officer should, from a date so agreed, assume responsibility for co-ordinating the provision of the after-care services to be so provided.

(3) The persons referred to in subsection (1) above are—

    (a) the patient and, if practicable and the patient does not object, his nearest relative;

    (b) the other persons concerned or to be concerned with the patient's medical treatment (including the new special medical officer);

    (c) the patient's after-care officer;

    (d) the other persons professionally concerned or to be so concerned with any aspect of the after-care services provided or to be provided for the patient under section 8 of this Act; and

    (e) any person who the special medical officer believes plays or is to play a substantial part in the care of the patient but is not, and will not be, professionally concerned with the after-care services so provided or to be so provided.

(4) The persons referred to in subsection (2) above are—

    (a) the patient and, if practicable and the patient does not object, his nearest relative;

    (b) the patient's special medical officer;

    (c) the other persons concerned or to be concerned with the patient's medical treatment;

    (d) the other persons professionally concerned or to be so concerned with any aspect of the after-care services provided or to be provided for the patient under section 8 of this Act (including the new after-care officer); and

    (e) any person who the after-care officer believes plays or is to play a substantial part in the care of the patient but is not, and will not be, professionally concerned with the after-care services so provided or to be so provided.

(5) If the patient has a propensity to violent or dangerous behaviour the special medical officer or, as the case may be, the after-care officer may consult the patient's nearest relative notwithstanding any objection by the patient to such consultation under subsection (3)(a) or, as the case may be, (4)(a) above.

(6) Where subsection (1) or (2) above applies the new special medical officer or, as the case may be, the new after-care officer shall, from the agreed date, assume responsibility as mentioned in that subsection and shall within seven days of that date intimate the change, in the prescribed form, to—

(a) the patient and any other person who has been consulted under paragraph (a) or (e) of subsection (3) or, as the case may be, (4) above or subsection (5) above;

(b) the Mental Welfare Commission; and

(c) the patient's after-care officer or, as the case may be, special medical officer.

(7) On a change of special medical officer or after-care officer by virtue of this section, the community care order shall have effect in respect of the patient as if the new special medical officer or, as the case may be, the new after-care officer had been the special medical officer or after-care officer specified in the community care order by virtue of section 35A(4) of this Act.

Appeal against community care order.

35F.—(1) Any patient subject to a community care order may, at any time when the order is in force following renewal under section 35C(5) of this Act, appeal to the sheriff for revocation of the order.

(2) An appeal under subsection (1) above shall be by way of summary application and shall be made to the sheriff of the sheriffdom within which the patient is resident.

(3) On an appeal under subsection (1) above—

(a) if the sheriff is satisfied that the patient—

(i) does not require to be subject to a community care order with a view to ensuring that he receives medical treatment and after-care services provided for him under section 8 of this Act; and

(ii) does not require to be subject to such an order in the interests of his health or safety or with a view to the protection of other persons,

he shall revoke the order; and

(b) in any other case, the sheriff shall refuse the appeal and affirm the order, either without amendment or subject to such variation as he considers appropriate.

(4) Where, under subsection (3)(a) above, the sheriff revokes a community care order he may order that the revocation shall have effect either immediately or from such date, not later than 28 days after the date of his decision, as he may specify.

(5) The special medical officer shall notify the patient's after-care officer of any revocation or variation of a community care order under this section.

Admission to hospital for reassessment.

35G.—(1) This section applies where, as respects a patient in respect of whom a community care order is in force, the special medical officer, after consulting the persons mentioned in subsection (2) below, considers that the patient's mental condition—

    (a) has, since the making of the order or, where the order has been renewed under section 35C(5) of this Act, the most recent renewal, deteriorated; and

    (b) is, or is likely to become, such as to give grounds for serious concern regarding his health or safety or the protection of other persons.

(2) The persons referred to in subsection (1) above are—

    (a) if practicable and the patient does not object, his nearest relative;

    (b) the other persons concerned with the patient's medical treatment;

    (c) the patient's after-care officer;

    (d) the other persons professionally concerned with any aspect of the after-care services provided for the patient under section 8 of this Act; and

    (e) any person who the special medical officer believes plays a substantial part in the care of the patient but is not professionally concerned with the after-care services so provided.

(3) If the patient has a propensity to violent or dangerous behaviour the special medical officer may consult the patient's nearest relative notwithstanding any objection by the patient to such consultation under subsection (2)(a) above.

(4) Where this section applies, the special medical officer shall—

    (a) examine the patient and prepare a report on his condition; and

    (b) arrange for another medical practitioner to carry out such an examination and provide such a report.

(5) Where both reports conclude that—

    (a) the patient is suffering from mental disorder of a nature or degree which makes it appropriate for him to be admitted to and detained in a hospital for assessment, or for assessment followed by medical treatment, for at least a limited period; and

    (b) he ought to be so admitted and detained in the interests of his own health or safety or with a view to the protection of other persons,

the special medical officer may, with the consent of the patient's after-care officer, direct the patient to attend a hospital specified in the direction to be admitted and detained there by virtue of this section, and the direction shall be sufficient authority for the patient's removal to the hospital so specified and for his admission to and detention in that hospital in accordance with this section.

(6) Reports under subsection (4) above and directions under subsection (5) above shall be in the prescribed form.

(7) The special medical officer shall send a copy of the reports under subsection (4) above and of the direction under subsection (5) above to—

(a) any person who has been consulted under subsection (2)(a) or (e) or (3) above;

(b) the Mental Welfare Commission;

(c) the managers of the hospital specified in the direction; and

(d) the patient's after-care officer.

(8) Subject to section 35H(4)(b) of this Act, a patient admitted to a hospital by virtue of this section may be detained there for a period not exceeding 7 days beginning with the day on which he is admitted and shall not be further detained in a hospital by virtue of this section immediately after the expiry of the period of detention.

(9) While a patient is detained in a hospital by virtue of this section the period for which, under section 35C of this Act, the community care order has effect shall continue to run but the conditions to which he is subject under the order shall not apply in relation to him.

Reassessment: further provisions.

35H.—(1) Where a patient is detained in a hospital by virtue of section 35G of this Act, the responsible medical officer shall—

(a) examine the patient and prepare a report, in the prescribed form, on his condition; and

(b) arrange for another medical practitioner to carry out such an examination and provide such a report.

(2) If the responsible medical officer is not a practitioner approved for the purposes of section 20 of this Act by a Health Board as having special experience in the diagnosis or treatment of mental disorder, the medical practitioner referred to in subsection (1)(b) above shall require to be such a practitioner.

(3) Where both reports conclude that the conditions set out in section 35B(8)(a) and (b) of this Act apply in relation to the patient, the patient shall, as soon as is practicable, be discharged from hospital and the conditions to which he is subject under the community care order shall again apply in relation to him.

(4) Where both reports conclude that the grounds set out in section 17(1)(a) and (b) of this Act apply in relation to the patient and, within the period specified in section 35G(8) of this Act, an application for admission is made in respect of the patient—

(a) the community care order in respect of the patient shall cease to have effect; and

(b) the submission to the sheriff, in accordance with section 21(1) of this Act, of the application for admission shall be sufficient authority for the detention of the patient in a hospital until the expiry of a further period of 21 days immediately following the expiry of the period specified in section 35G(8).

(5) The responsible medical officer shall send to the Mental Welfare Commission copies of the reports prepared under subsection (1) above.

(6) A patient detained in a hospital by virtue of section 35G of this Act shall cease to be liable to be so detained, and the community care order in respect of him shall cease to have effect—

(a) if the period mentioned in subsection (8) of that section expires without the patient having been discharged from hospital or an application for his admission having been submitted to the sheriff; or

(b) where an application for his admission has been submitted to the sheriff within that period, if the period of 21 days mentioned in subsection (4)(b) above expires without the sheriff having approved the application.

(7) For the purposes of this section, an application for admission is submitted to the sheriff when it is lodged with his sheriff clerk.

Revocation of community care order.

35I.—(1) Where the special medical officer, after consulting the persons mentioned in subsection (2) below, considers that the patient—

(a) does not require to be subject to a community care order with a view to ensuring that he receives medical treatment and after-care services provided for him under section 8 of this Act; and

(b) does not require to be subject to such an order in the interests of his health or safety or with a view to the protection of other persons,

he shall revoke the order and shall notify the patient, his nearest relative (if practicable), his after-care officer, any person falling within subsection (2)(e) below and the Mental Welfare Commission of the revocation.

(2) The persons to be consulted under subsection (1) above are—

(a) the patient and, if practicable and the patient does not object, his nearest relative;

(b) the other persons concerned with the patient's medical treatment;

(c) the patient's after-care officer;

(d) the other persons professionally concerned with any aspect of the after-care services provided for the patient under section 8 of this Act; and

(e) any person who the special medical officer believes plays a substantial part in the care of the patient but is not professionally concerned with the after-care services so provided.

(3) If the patient has a propensity to violent or dangerous behaviour the special medical officer may consult the patient's nearest relative notwithstanding any objection by the patient to such consultation under subsection (2)(a) above.

(4) Where the Mental Welfare Commission consider that the patient—

(a) does not require to be subject to a community care order with a view to ensuring that he receives medical treatment and after-care services provided for him under section 8 of this Act; and

(b) does not require to be subject to such an order in the interests of his health or safety or with a view to the protection of other persons,

they shall revoke the order and shall notify the persons mentioned in subsection (5) below of the revocation.

(5) The persons to be notified under subsection (4) above are—

(a) the patient and (if practicable) his nearest relative;

(b) the patient's special medical officer;

(c) the patient's after-care officer; and

(d) any person who the Mental Welfare Commission believes plays a substantial part in the care of the patient but is not professionally concerned with the after-care services provided for the patient under section 8 of this Act.

Patients in custody or admitted to hospital in pursuance of emergency recommendations.

35J.—(1) This section applies where a patient who is subject to a community care order—

(a) is detained in custody in pursuance of any sentence or order passed or made by a court in the United Kingdom (including an order committing or remanding him in custody); or

(b) is detained in a hospital under section 24, 26 or 26A of this Act.

(2) For so long as the patient is detained as mentioned in subsection (1)(a) or (b) above the period for which, under section 35C of this Act, the community care order has effect shall continue to run but the conditions to which he is subject under that order shall not apply in relation to him.

(3) If the patient is detained as mentioned in paragraph (a) of subsection (1) above for a period of, or successive periods amounting in the aggregate to, 6 months or less, or is detained as mentioned in paragraph (b) of that subsection, and, apart from this subsection, the community care order—

(a) would have ceased to have effect during the period for which he is so detained; or

(b) would cease to have effect during the period of 28 days beginning with the day on which he ceases to be so detained,

the order shall be deemed not to have ceased, and shall not cease, to have effect until the end of that period of 28 days.

(4) Where the period for which the patient is subject to a community care order is extended by subsection (3) above, any examination and report to be made and furnished in respect of the patient under section 35C(3) and (5) of this Act may be made and furnished within the period as so extended.

(5) Where, by virtue of subsection (4) above, a community care order is renewed for a further period after the day on which (apart from subsection (3) above) the order would have ceased to have effect, the further period shall be deemed to have commenced with that day.

Patients moving from England and Wales to Scotland.

35K.—(1) A community care application may be made in respect of a patient who is subject to after-care under supervision under the Mental Health Act 1983 and who intends to leave England and Wales in order to reside in Scotland. 1983 c. 20.

(2) Sections 35A to 35J of this Act shall apply in relation to a patient in respect of whom a community care application is or is to be made by virtue of this section subject to such modifications as may be prescribed."

(2) Schedule 2 to this Act (supplementary provisions about community care orders) shall have effect.

Absence without leave. 1984 c. 36.

5.—(1) In section 28 of the Mental Health (Scotland) Act 1984 (return of hospital patients absent without leave), for subsection (3) (which provides that a patient may not be taken into custody after the end of the period of 28 days beginning with the first day of his absence without leave) there shall be substituted the following subsection—

"(3) A patient shall not be taken into custody under this section after the later of—

(a) the end of the period of six months beginning with the first day of his absence without leave; and

(b) the end of the period for which (apart from section 31 of this Act) he is liable to be detained;

and, in determining for the purposes of paragraph (b) above or any other provision of this Act whether a person who is or has been absent without leave is at any time liable to be detained, a report furnished under section 30 or 31B of this Act before the first day of his absence shall not be taken to have renewed the authority for his detention unless the period of renewal began before that day."

(2) In section 30(6) of that Act (right of appeal where authority for detention renewed), after the word "section" where it first occurs there shall be inserted "or section 31B of this Act".

(3) For section 31 of that Act (duration of authority for detention: special provisions as to patients absent without leave) there shall be substituted the following sections—

"Special provisions as to patients absent without leave: hospital.

31.—(1) Where a patient is absent without leave—

   (a) on the day on which (apart from this section) he would cease to be liable to be detained under this Part of this Act; or

   (b) within the period of one week ending with that day,

he shall not cease to be so liable until the relevant time.

(2) For the purposes of subsection (1) above the relevant time—

   (a) where the patient is taken into custody under section 28 of this Act, is the end of the period of one week beginning with the day on which he is returned to the hospital;

   (b) where the patient returns to the hospital within the period during which he can be taken into custody under section 28 of this Act, is the end of the period of one week beginning with the day on which he so returns; and

   (c) otherwise, is the end of the period during which he can be taken into custody under section 28 of this Act.

Patients who are taken into custody or return within 28 days: hospital.

31A.—(1) This section applies where a patient who is absent without leave is taken into custody under section 28 of this Act, or returns to the hospital, not later than the end of the period of 28 days beginning with the first day of his absence without leave.

(2) Where the period for which the patient is liable to be detained is extended by section 31 of this Act, any examination and report to be made and furnished in respect of the patient under section 30(3) of this Act may be made and furnished within the period as so extended.

(3) Where the authority for the detention of a patient is renewed by virtue of subsection (2) above after the day on which (apart from section 31 of this Act) that authority would have expired, the renewal shall take effect as from that day.

Patients who are taken into custody or return after more than 28

31B.—(1) This section applies where a patient who is absent without leave is taken into custody under section 28 of this Act, or returns to the hospital, later than the end of the period of 28 days beginning with the first day of his absence without leave.

days: hospital.

(2) The responsible medical officer shall, within the period of one week beginning with the day on which the patient returns, or is returned, to the hospital—

(a) examine the patient or obtain from another medical practitioner a report on the condition of the patient; and

(b) consult—

(i) such other person or persons who appear to him to be principally concerned with the patient's medical treatment; and

(ii) a mental health officer,

and thereafter assess the need for the detention of the patient to be continued; and if it appears to him that the grounds set out in section 17(1) of this Act apply to the patient he shall furnish to the managers of the hospital where the patient is liable to be detained and to the Mental Welfare Commission a report to that effect in the prescribed form, along with the report first mentioned if such a report has been obtained.

(3) Where a report under this section is furnished to them in respect of a patient, the managers of a hospital shall, unless they discharge the patient, cause him and his nearest relative to be informed.

(4) Where the patient would (apart from any renewal of the authority for his detention on or after the day on which he is returned or returns to the hospital) be liable to be detained after the end of the period of one week beginning with that day, he shall cease to be so liable at the end of that period unless a report is duly furnished in respect of him under subsection (2) above.

(5) Where the patient would (apart from section 31 of this Act) have ceased to be liable to be detained on or before the day on which a report is duly furnished in respect of him under subsection (2) above, the report shall renew the authority for his detention for the period prescribed in that case by section 30(2) of this Act.

(6) Where the authority for the detention of the patient is renewed by virtue of subsection (5) above—

(a) the renewal shall take effect as from the day on which (apart from section 31 of this Act and subsection (5) above) the authority would have expired; and

(b) if (apart from this paragraph) the renewed authority would expire on or before the day on which the report is furnished, the report shall further renew the authority, as from the day on which it would expire, for the period prescribed in that case by section 30(2) of this Act.

(7) Where the authority for the detention of the patient would expire within the period of two months beginning with the day on which a report is duly furnished in respect

of him under subsection (2) above, the report shall, if it so provides, have effect also as a report duly furnished under section 30(3) of this Act; and the reference in this subsection to authority includes any authority renewed under subsection (5) above by the report."

(4) In section 32 of that Act (special provisions as to patients sentenced to imprisonment etc: hospital)—

    (a) in subsection (2) (detained person in whose case application for admission does not cease to have effect), for the words "and 31" there shall be substituted ", 31 and 31A"; and

    (b) after that subsection there shall be inserted the following subsection—

        "(3) In its application by virtue of subsection (2) above section 28(3) of this Act shall have effect with the substitution of the words "end of the period of 28 days beginning with the first day of his absence without leave." for the words from "later of" onwards."

(5) In section 44 of that Act (return of patients subject to guardianship absent without leave), for subsection (2) (which provides that a patient may not be taken into custody after the end of the period of 28 days beginning with the first day of his absence without leave) there shall be substituted the following subsections—

    "(2) A patient shall not be taken into custody under this section after the later of—

    (a) the end of the period of six months beginning with the first day of his absence without leave; and

    (b) the end of the period for which (apart from section 48 of this Act) he is subject to guardianship;

and, in determining for the purposes of paragraph (b) above or any other provision of this Act whether a person who is or has been absent without leave is at any time subject to guardianship, a report furnished under section 47 or 48B of this Act before the first day of his absence shall not be taken to have renewed the authority for his guardianship unless the period of renewal began before that day."

(6) In section 47(6) of that Act (right of appeal where authority for guardianship renewed), after the word "section" where it first occurs there shall be inserted "or section 48B of this Act".

(7) For section 48 of that Act (duration of authority for guardianship: special provisions as to patients absent without leave) there shall be substituted the following sections—

"Special provisions as to patients absent without leave: guardianship.

48.—(1) Where a patient is absent without leave—

    (a) on the day on which (apart from this section) he would cease to be subject to guardianship under this Part of this Act; or

    (b) within the period of one week ending with that day,

he shall not cease to be so subject until the relevant time.

    (2) For the purposes of subsection (1) above the relevant time—

(a) where the patient is taken into custody under section 44 of this Act, is the end of the period of one week beginning with the day on which he is returned to the place where he ought to be;

(b) where the patient returns to the place where he ought to be within the period during which he can be taken into custody under section 44 of this Act, is the end of the period of one week beginning with the day on which he so returns; and

(c) otherwise, is the end of the period during which he can be taken into custody under section 44 of this Act.

Patients who are taken into custody or return within 28 days: guardianship.

48A.—(1) This section applies where a patient who is absent without leave is taken into custody under section 44 of this Act, or returns to the place where he ought to be, not later than the end of the period of 28 days beginning with the first day of his absence without leave.

(2) Where the period for which the patient is subject to guardianship is extended by section 48 of this Act, any examination and report to be made and furnished in respect of the patient under section 47(3) of this Act may be made and furnished within the period as so extended.

(3) Where the authority for the guardianship of a patient is renewed by virtue of subsection (2) above after the day on which (apart from section 44 of this Act) that authority would have expired, the renewal shall take effect as from that day.

Patients who are taken into custody or return after more than 28 days: guardianship.

48B.—(1) This section applies where a patient who is absent without leave is taken into custody under section 44 of this Act, or returns to the place where he ought to be, later than the end of the period of 28 days beginning with the first day of his absence without leave.

(2) Within the period of one week beginning with the day on which the patient returns, or is returned, to the place where he ought to be—

(a) the responsible medical officer shall examine the patient or obtain from another medical practitioner a report on the condition of the patient; and, if it appears to him that the ground set out in section 36(a) of this Act continues to apply in relation to the patient, he shall furnish to such mental health officer as the local authority concerned may direct a report to that effect in the prescribed form, along with the report first mentioned if such a report has been obtained; and

(b) the mental health officer shall consider whether the ground set out in section 36(a) of this Act continues to apply in relation to the patient; and, if it appears to him it does continue so to apply, he shall furnish to the local authority concerned and to the Mental Welfare Commission a report to that effect in the prescribed form along with the report or reports furnished to him under paragraph (a) of this subsection.

(3) Where a report under this section is furnished to them in respect of a patient, the local authority shall, unless they discharge the patient, cause him, his nearest relative and his guardian to be informed.

(4) Where the patient would (apart from any renewal of the authority for his guardianship on or after the day on which he is returned or returns to the place where he ought to be) be subject to guardianship after the end of the period of one week beginning with that day, he shall cease to be so subject at the end of that period unless a report is duly furnished in respect of him under subsection (2) above.

(5) Where the patient would (apart from section 48 of this Act) have ceased to be subject to guardianship on or before the day on which a report is duly furnished in respect of him under subsection (2) above, the report shall renew the authority for his guardianship for the period prescribed in that case by section 47(2) of this Act.

(6) Where the authority for the guardianship of the patient is renewed by virtue of subsection (5) above—

(a) the renewal shall take effect as from the day on which (apart from section 48 of this Act and subsection (5) above) the authority would have expired; and

(b) if (apart from this paragraph) the renewed authority would expire on or before the day on which the report is furnished, the report shall further renew the authority, as from the day on which it would expire, for the period prescribed in that case by section 47(2) of this Act.

(7) Where the authority for the guardianship of the patient would expire within the period of two months beginning with the day on which a report is duly furnished in respect of him under subsection (2) above, the report shall, if it so provides, have effect also as a report duly furnished under section 47(3) of this Act; and the reference in this subsection to authority includes any authority renewed under subsection (5) above by the report."

(8) In section 49 of that Act (special provisions as to patients sentenced to imprisonment etc: guardianship)—

(a) in subsection (2) (detained person in whose case guardianship application does not cease to have effect), for the words "and 48" there shall be substituted ", 48 and 48A"; and

(b) after that subsection there shall be inserted the following subsection—

"(3) In its application by virtue of subsection (2) above section 44(2) of this Act shall have effect with the substitution of the words "end of the period of 28 days beginning with the first day of his absence without leave." for the words from "later of" onwards.""

(9) In section 60 of that Act (effect of hospital orders), after subsection (4) there shall be inserted the following subsection—

"(5) Where—

(a) a patient admitted to a hospital in pursuance of a hospital order is absent without leave;

(b) a warrant to arrest him has been issued under section 13 of the Criminal Procedure (Scotland) Act 1975; and

(c) he is held pursuant to the warrant in any country or territory other than the United Kingdom, any of the Channel Islands and the Isle of Man,

he shall be treated as having been taken into custody under section 28 of this Act on first being so held."

1975 c. 21.

(10) In section 99 of that Act (review of treatment), in subsection (1) (report on treatment and patient's condition to be given to Mental Welfare Commission), in paragraph (a) (report to be given when report furnished under section 30), for the words "in respect of the patient under section 30 of this Act" there shall be substituted "under section 30 or 31B of this Act renewing the authority for the detention of the patient".

(11) In Schedule 2 to that Act (application of Part V to patients subject to hospital or guardianship orders)—

(a) in paragraph 1 of Part I (provisions applying without modifications to patients subject to hospital order without restriction or transfer order without restriction), after "31" there shall be inserted "to 31B"; and

(b) in paragraph 1 of Part III (provisions applying without modifications to patients subject to guardianship), after "48" there shall be inserted "to 48B".

6.—(1) Section 27 of the Mental Health (Scotland) Act 1984 (leave of absence from hospital) shall be amended in accordance with subsections (2) and (3) below.

Leave of absence from hospital.
1984 c. 36.

(2) In subsection (2), after the word "may" in the second place where it occurs there shall be inserted ", subject to subsection (2A) below,".

(3) After subsection (2) there shall be inserted the following subsections—

"(2A) Subject to subsections (2B) and (2C) below, the total period of leave of absence for specified consecutive periods under this section shall not exceed 12 months.

(2B) If, on the date of expiry of leave of absence granted to a patient under this section, a community care application has been made in respect of him but has not been determined, the leave of absence shall continue until the community care order comes into force or, as the case may be, the application is refused by the sheriff.

(2C) If, on the date of expiry of leave of absence granted to a patient under this section, a community care order has been made in respect of him but has not come into force, the leave of absence shall continue until the order comes into force."

(4) In paragraph 4 of Part II of Schedule 2 to that Act (application of section 27 to hospital orders with restriction orders, etc.), at the end of sub-paragraph (b) there shall be inserted the following sub-paragraph—

"(bb) subsections (2A) to (2C) shall be omitted;".

(5) Where, on the day when this section comes into force, a patient has been absent from a hospital for more than 6 months in pursuance of leave of absence granted under section 27 of that Act, the leave may, notwithstanding subsection (3) above, be extended for a single period of not more than 6 months.

Supplementary

Short title, commencement and extent.

7.—(1) This Act may be cited as the Mental Health (Patients in the Community) Act 1995.

(2) This Act shall come into force on 1st April 1996.

(3) The provisions of this Act which amend other enactments have the same extent as the enactments which they amend.

SCHEDULES

SCHEDULE 1   Section 1(2).

AFTER-CARE UNDER SUPERVISION: SUPPLEMENTARY

Records

1. In section 24 of the Mental Health Act 1983 (visiting and examination of   1983 c. 20.
patients), in each of subsections (2) and (4) (records) at the end there shall be
inserted the words "or to any after-care services provided for the patient under
section 117 below."

Regulations

2. In section 32 of that Act (regulations for purposes of Part II), in subsection
(2)(c) (records etc.)—

   (a) for the words "the managers of hospitals and local social services
   authorities" there shall be substituted "such bodies as may be
   prescribed by the regulations";

   (b) for the words "prescribed by the regulations" there shall be substituted
   "so prescribed"; and

   (c) after the word "guardianship" there shall be inserted "or to after-care
   under supervision".

Wards of court

3. In section 33 of that Act (wards of court), at the end there shall be inserted
the following subsection—

   "(4) Where a supervision application has been made in respect of a
   minor who is a ward of court, the provisions of this Part of this Act relating
   to after-care under supervision have effect in relation to the minor subject
   to any order which the court may make in the exercise of its wardship
   jurisdiction."

Medical officers and supervisors

4.—(1) Section 34 of that Act (interpretation) shall be amended in accordance
with sub-paragraphs (2) to (5) below.

(2) In subsection (1), before the definition of "the nominated medical
attendant" there shall be inserted the following definition—

   ""the community responsible medical officer", in relation to a patient
   subject to after-care under supervision, means the person who, in
   accordance with section 117(2A)(a) below, is in charge of medical
   treatment provided for him;".

(3) In that subsection, in the definition of "the responsible medical officer"—

   (a) after the word "means" there shall be inserted "(except in the phrase
   "the community responsible medical officer")"; and

   (b) in paragraph (a), after the words "a patient" there shall be inserted
   "who is" and after the words "admission for treatment" there shall be
   inserted "or who is to be subject to after-care under supervision after
   leaving hospital".

(4) In that subsection, after the definition of "the responsible medical officer",
there shall be inserted the following definition—

   ""the supervisor", in relation to a patient subject to after-care under
   supervision, means the person who, in accordance with section
   117(2A)(b) below, is supervising him."

(5) After that subsection there shall be inserted the following subsection—

"(1A) Nothing in this Act prevents the same person from acting as more than one of the following in relation to a patient, that is—

(a) the responsible medical officer;

(b) the community responsible medical officer; and

(c) the supervisor."

Part III patients

5. In section 41 of that Act (power of higher courts to restrict discharge from hospital of persons subject to hospital order), in subsection (3) (nature of special restrictions), after paragraph (a) there shall be inserted the following paragraph—

"(aa) none of the provisions of Part II of this Act relating to after-care under supervision shall apply;".

6. In Schedule 1 to that Act (application of provisions to patients subject to hospital and guardianship orders), in Part I (patients not subject to special restrictions)—

(a) in paragraph 1 (provisions applying without modification), for "26" there shall be substituted "25C";

(b) in paragraph 2 (provisions applying with modifications), after "23" there shall be inserted ", 25A, 25B"; and

(c) after paragraph 8 there shall be inserted the following paragraph—

"8A. In sections 25A(1)(a) and 25B(5)(a) for the words "in pursuance of an application for admission for treatment" there shall be substituted the words "by virtue of an order or direction for his admission or removal to hospital under Part III of this Act"."

Mental Health Review Tribunals

7.—(1) Section 66 of that Act (applications to tribunals) shall be amended in accordance with sub-paragraphs (2) to (4) below.

(2) In subsection (1) (cases where application may be made), after paragraph (g) there shall be inserted the following paragraphs—

"(ga) a supervision application is accepted in respect of a patient; or

(gb) a report is furnished under section 25F above in respect of a patient; or

(gc) a report is furnished under section 25G above in respect of a patient; or".

(3) In that subsection, in paragraph (i), for the words "case mentioned in paragraph (d) above, by his nearest relative" there shall be substituted "cases mentioned in paragraphs (d), (ga), (gb) and (gc), by his nearest relative if he has been (or was entitled to be) informed under this Act of the report or acceptance".

(4) In subsection (2) (period within which application may be made)—

(a) in paragraph (c), for the words "case mentioned in paragraph (c)" there shall be substituted "cases mentioned in paragraphs (c) and (ga)";

(b) in paragraph (d), for the words "and (g)" there shall be substituted ", (g) and (gb)"; and

(c) after paragraph (f) there shall be inserted the following paragraph—

"(fa) in the case mentioned in paragraph (gc) of that subsection, the further period for which the patient is made subject to after-care under supervision by virtue of the report;".

8.—(1) Section 67 of that Act (references to tribunals by Secretary of State) shall be amended in accordance with sub-paragraphs (2) and (3) below.

(2) In subsection (1) (power of Secretary of State to refer), after the word "guardianship" there shall be inserted "or to after-care under supervision".

(3) In subsection (2) (power of registered medical practitioner to require records), at the end there shall be inserted the words "or to any after-care services provided for the patient under section 117 below".

9. In section 68 of that Act (duty of managers of hospitals to refer cases to tribunal), in subsection (3) (power of registered medical practitioner to require records), at the end there shall be inserted the words "or to any after-care services provided for the patient under section 117 below".

10.—(1) Section 72 of that Act (powers of tribunal) shall be amended in accordance with sub-paragraphs (2) to (4) below.

(2) After subsection (3) there shall be inserted the following subsection—

"(3A) Where, in the case of an application to a tribunal by or in respect of a patient who is liable to be detained in pursuance of an application for admission for treatment or by virtue of an order or direction for his admission or removal to hospital under Part III of this Act, the tribunal do not direct the discharge of the patient under subsection (1) above, the tribunal may—

(a) recommend that the responsible medical officer consider whether to make a supervision application in respect of the patient; and

(b) further consider his case in the event of no such application being made."

(3) After subsection (4) there shall be inserted the following subsection—

"(4A) Where application is made to a Mental Health Review Tribunal by or in respect of a patient who is subject to after-care under supervision (or, if he has not yet left hospital, is to be so subject after he leaves hospital), the tribunal may in any case direct that the patient shall cease to be so subject (or not become so subject), and shall so direct if they are satisfied—

(a) in a case where the patient has not yet left hospital, that the conditions set out in section 25A(4) above are not complied with; or

(b) in any other case, that the conditions set out in section 25G(4) above are not complied with."

(4) In subsection (5) (power of tribunal to amend application, order or direction where satisfied that patient is suffering from a form of mental disorder different from that specified in it), after the word "discharged" there shall be inserted "or, if he is (or is to be) subject to after-care under supervision, that he cease to be so subject (or not become so subject)".

11. In section 76(1) of that Act (visiting and examination of patients)—

(a) after the word "guardianship" there shall be inserted "or to after-care under supervision (or, if he has not yet left hospital, is to be subject to after-care under supervision after he leaves hospital)"; and

(b) in paragraph (b), at the end there shall be inserted the words "or to any after-care services provided for the patient under section 117 below."

12. In section 77(3) of that Act (tribunal applications), after the word "guardianship" there shall be inserted "or when subject to after-care under supervision (or in which he is to reside on becoming so subject after leaving hospital)".

13. In section 79(6) of that Act (interpretation of Part V), after the words "a hospital" there shall be inserted ", and "the responsible medical officer" means the responsible medical officer,".

14. In Schedule 1 to that Act (application of provisions to patients subject to hospital and guardianship orders), in Part I (patients not subject to special restrictions), in paragraph 9(b) (modifications of section 66(2)), for the words from "shall be omitted" to the end there shall be substituted ", and in paragraph (d) ", (g)", shall be omitted."

After-care services

15.—(1) Section 117 of that Act (after-care services) shall be amended in accordance with sub-paragraphs (2) to (4) below.

(2) In subsection (1) (persons to whom section 117 applies), after the words "detained and" there shall be inserted "(whether or not immediately after so ceasing)".

(3) In subsection (2) (duty of authorities to provide after-care services), at the end there shall be inserted the words "; but they shall not be so satisfied in the case of a patient who is subject to after-care under supervision at any time while he remains so subject."

(4) After that subsection there shall be inserted the following subsections—

"(2A) It shall be the duty of the Health Authority to secure that at all times while a patient is subject to after-care under supervision—

(a) a person who is a registered medical practitioner approved for the purposes of section 12 above by the Secretary of State as having special experience in the diagnosis or treatment of mental disorder is in charge of the medical treatment provided for the patient as part of the after-care services provided for him under this section; and

(b) a person professionally concerned with any of the after-care services so provided is supervising him with a view to securing that he receives the after-care services so provided.

(2B) Section 32 above shall apply for the purposes of this section as it applies for the purposes of Part II of this Act."

Code of practice

16. In section 118 of that Act (code of practice), in subsection (1)(a) (guidance to medical practitioners, social workers etc.), after the word "Act" there shall be inserted "and to guardianship and after-care under supervision under this Act".

Offences

17. In section 126 of that Act (forgery, false statements etc.), in subsection (3)(b) (subsection (1) to apply to medical recommendations and reports), after the word "medical" there shall be inserted "or other".

18. In section 127 of that Act (ill-treatment of patients), after subsection (2) there shall be inserted the following subsection—

"(2A) It shall be an offence for any individual to ill-treat or wilfully to neglect a mentally disordered patient who is for the time being subject to after-care under supervision."

19. In section 129 of that Act (obstruction), in subsection (1)(b) (refusal to allow visiting, interviewing or examination by a person authorised by or under the Act), after the word "Act" there shall be inserted "or to give access to any person to a person so authorised".

Interpretation

20.—(1) Section 145 of that Act (interpretation) shall be amended in accordance with sub-paragraphs (2) and (3) below.

(2) In subsection (1)—

    (a) after the definition of "patient" there shall be inserted the following definition—

        ""the responsible after-care bodies" has the meaning given in section 25D above;"; and

    (b) after the definition of "special hospital" there shall be inserted the following definition—

        ""supervision application" has the meaning given in section 25A above;".

(3) After that subsection there shall be inserted the following subsection—

    "(1A) References in this Act to a patient being subject to after-care under supervision (or to after-care under supervision) shall be construed in accordance with section 25A above."

SCHEDULE 2

Section 4(2).

COMMUNITY CARE ORDERS: SUPPLEMENTARY

Mental Welfare Commission

1. In section 3 of the Mental Health (Scotland) Act 1984 (functions and duties of Mental Welfare Commission), in each of subsections (1) and (2)(b), after the word "guardianship" there shall be inserted "or a community care order".

1984 c. 36.

2. In section 5 of that Act (duties of Secretary of State and local authorities in relation to Mental Welfare Commission), after subsection (2) there shall be inserted the following subsection—

    "(3) The local authority providing after-care services under section 8 of this Act for a patient subject to a community care order shall afford the Mental Welfare Commission all facilities necessary to carry out their functions in relation to such a patient."

After-care services

3. In section 8(1) of that Act (duty of local authority to provide after-care services), at the end there shall be inserted the words "and shall (without prejudice to the foregoing) provide or arrange for the provision of after-care services for any person who is subject to a community care order".

Part VI patients

4. In section 62 of that Act (application of Act to patients subject to restriction orders), in subsection (1), after paragraph (a) there shall be inserted the following paragraph—

    "(aa) none of the provisions of Part V of this Act relating to community care orders shall apply;".

5. In Schedule 2 to that Act (application of Part V to patients subject to hospital or guardianship orders), in Part I (hospital order without restriction order and transfer order without restriction)—

  (a) in paragraph 1 (provisions applying without modification), after "32," there shall be inserted "35A,";

  (b) in paragraph 2 (provisions applying with modifications), after "35," there shall be inserted "35B,"; and

  (c) after paragraph 8 there shall be inserted the following paragraph—

    "8A. In section 35B(1) for the words "an application for admission" there shall be substituted the words "an order or direction by virtue of which he is liable under Part VI of this Act to be detained.""

Offences

6. In section 105 of that Act (ill-treatment of patients), after subsection (2) there shall be inserted the following subsection—

  "(2A) It shall be an offence for any individual to ill-treat or wilfully neglect a patient in respect of whom a community care order is for the time being in force."

7. In section 109 of that Act (obstruction), in subsection (1), after the word "Act," there shall be inserted "or to give access to any person to a person so authorised".

Duty to inform nearest relative

8. In section 111(1) of that Act (duty of managers of hospital to inform nearest relative of discharge of patient), after the words "nearest relative" in the first place where they occur there shall be inserted "or the making of a community care order".

Code of practice

9. In section 119 of that Act (code of practice), in subsection (1)(a) (guidance to medical practitioners, mental health officers etc.), after the word "Act" there shall be inserted "guardianship under this Act and after-care services provided under section 8 of this Act for patients subject to community care orders".

Interpretation

10. In section 125(1) of that Act (interpretation), the following definitions shall be inserted in the appropriate places in alphabetical order—

  ""after-care officer" has the meaning assigned to it by section 35A(4)(c) of this Act;";

  ""community care application" and "community care order" have the meanings respectively assigned to them by section 35A(1) of this Act;";

  ""special medical officer" has the meaning assigned to it by section 35A(4)(b) of this Act".

PRINTED IN THE UNITED KINGDOM BY MIKE LYNN
Controller and Chief Executive of Her Majesty's Stationery Office
and Queen's Printer of Acts of Parliament